DATE DUE

NO 3 '98			
GAYLORD			PRINTED IN U.S.A.

MAASAI

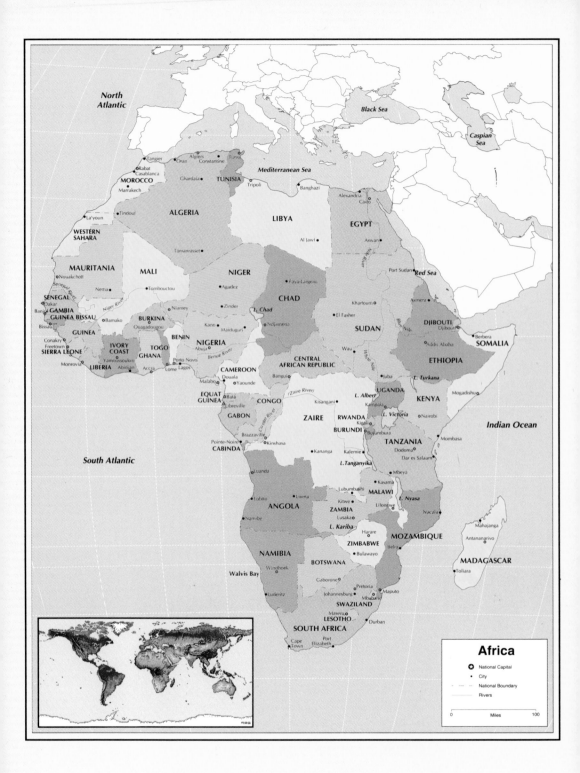

Africa

⊛ National Capital

• City

--- National Boundary

— Rivers

| 0 | Miles | 100 |

The Heritage Library of African Peoples

MAASAI

Tiyambe Zeleza, Ph.D.

THE ROSEN PUBLISHING GROUP, INC.
NEW YORK

Published in 1994 by The Rosen Publishing Group, Inc.
29 East 21st Street, New York, NY 10010

First Edition

Manufactured in the United States of America

Library of Congress Cataloging-in-Publication Data

Zeleza, Tiyambe.
  The Maasai / Tiyambe Zeleza. — 1st ed.
    p.   cm. — (The Heritage library of African peoples)
  Includes bibliographical references and index.
  ISBN 0-8239-1757-6
  1. Masai (African people)—History—Juvenile literature.   2. Maasai (African people)—Social life and customs—Juvenile literature.
  I. Title.   II. Series.
  DT433.545.M33Z45   1994
  967.62′7004965—dc20   94-5058
                                                                CIP
                                                                 AC

Contents

INTRODUCTION

THERE IS EVERY REASON FOR US TO KNOW something about Africa and to understand its past and the way of life of its peoples. Africa is a rich continent that has for centuries provided the world with art, culture, labor, wealth, and natural resources. It has vast mineral deposits, fossil fuels, and commercial crops.

But perhaps most important is the fact that fossil evidence indicates that human beings originated in Africa. The earliest traces of human beings and their tools are almost two million years old. Their descendants have migrated throughout the world. To be human is to be of African descent.

The experiences of the peoples who stayed in Africa are as rich and as diverse as of those who established themselves elsewhere. This series of books describes their environment, their modes of subsistence, their relationships, and their customs and beliefs. The books present the variety of languages, histories, cultures, and religions that are to be found on the African continent. They demonstrate the historical linkages between African peoples and the way contemporary Africa has been affected by European colonial rule.

Africa is large, complex, and diverse. It encompasses an area of more than 11,700,000

6

square miles. The United States, Europe, and India could fit easily into it. The sheer size is an indication of the continent's great variety in geography, terrain, climate, flora, fauna, peoples, languages, and cultures.

Much of contemporary Africa has been shaped by European colonial rule, industrialization, urbanization, and the demands of a world economic system. For more than seventy years, large regions of Africa were ruled by Great Britain, France, Belgium, Portugal, and Spain. African peoples from various ethnic, linguistic, and cultural backgrounds were brought together to form colonial states.

For decades Africans struggled to gain their independence. It was not until after World War II that the colonial territories become independent African states. Today, almost all of Africa is ruled by Africans. Large numbers of Africans live in modern cities. Rural Africa is also being transformed, and yet its people still engage in many of their age-old customs and beliefs.

Contemporary circumstances and natural events have not always been kind to ordinary Africans. Today, however, new popular social movements and technological innovations pose great promise for future development.

George C. Bond
Institute of African Studies
Columbia University, New York City

A Maasai village chief.

chapter

1

THE MAASAI PEOPLE

THERE WAS ONCE A GROUP OF PEOPLE WHO traveled down from the north of Africa. They traveled until they could go no farther. They stopped in a basin below some high cliffs. But the land there was dry. There was not enough grass to feed the cattle, and not enough cattle to feed the children. The elders knew that they must take their people away from this place, but they did not know where to go.

One day they saw a bird with green grass in its beak, flying into the bare trees to build a nest. They watched as the bird soared high up into the cliffs to find lush leaves. The elders sent a few young men to climb up and see what lay beyond the cliffs. There they saw streams, green trees, and soft grasses. It was a land rich enough to feed cattle and people for a long time. But how were they to climb those steep rocks?

A huge ladder was built, and up this remarkable ladder climbed the entire village: men, women, chil-

dren, even cattle! Half of the population had reached the high ground when the ladder broke. The people who had climbed out first looked down and knew that it was much too dangerous to try to save the others. They began a new life and prospered in the rich land. They are the Maasai, and that is how they came to be separate from other peoples.

This is one story that the Maasai tell to explain how they became a people. The Maasai are legendary as warriors throughout Africa and the world.

The Maasai live in the Rift Valley of East Africa and in the highlands of central Kenya and northern Tanzania. They are a Maa-speaking people, like their neighbors the Samburu, Jemps, Arusha, and Parakuyo. Maa is the language of the peoples who live in the Nile River Basin.

Little is known about the origins of the Maasai. Some scholars believe they came from northern Africa. They arrived in present-day Kenya around the fifteenth century and settled in the lowlands west of Lake Turkana. From there they gradually moved southward.

The expansion of the Maasai occurred in waves over a long period. By 1800, Maasailand was a vast area of more than 77,000 square miles. The Maasai met many other peoples in the process. They drove some of these peoples away and accepted others into the community, becoming a mix of ethnic groups.

Children are extremely important to the Maasai.

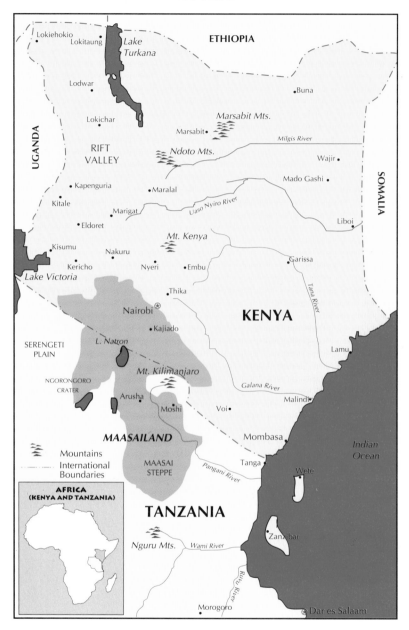

The many Maasai communities had different ways of life. Those who lived in the plains mostly kept cattle. They are called pastoralists, and are sometimes considered the "real" Maasai.

12

Many people view the Maasai as a proud people.

Others who lived in the highlands were farmers.

Some people think that the Maasai are a "backward" people and that they should abandon their traditional customs and values. Others see them as a proud people who have not been corrupted by modern society. Many hold the view that the Maasai must either adapt to the modern world or die out.

This is not necessarily true. In the past, the Maasai made various adaptations to meet challenges. Today they are adapting in new ways. New cultural practices and values have emerged while many old ones remain.▲

chapter

2

MAASAILAND

THE ORGANIZATION OF MAASAI SOCIETY IS complex. The Maasai were divided into a number of alliances. Each alliance was made up of independent social and political units called *iloshon*. Each *iloshon* was, in turn, made up of several localities. Each locality consisted of several homesteads, or *inkangitie* (singular, *enkang'*), of several families.

The *iloshon* usually contained two zones: The dry-season pastures were in higher areas with enough rainfall year-round. The lower-lying pastures were generally short of water, but they were rich in minerals and salt licks (natural deposits of rock salt). Maasai herders moved regularly between the two zones according to the season.

An *enkang'* or Maasai village.

A Maasai hut.

▼ LIVESTOCK ▼

The Maasai and other livestock keepers in East Africa had to deal with the problem of tsetse flies. These flies infect both humans and cattle with a parasite that causes the fatal disease trypanosomiasis, or sleeping sickness. The Maasai either avoided the infested areas altogether or herded their cattle through at night when it was relatively safe.

Livestock was the most important possession to the Maasai. They kept cattle, sheep, and goats. Most families also owned a few donkeys, which were used mainly for transportation, although they were milked in hard times. Cattle were the most highly valued of their animals and were usually kept in large herds. Livestock in general played many roles in Maasai society. To have a large herd was to be wealthy. Livestock provided staple foods like milk and meat and were also a source of manure and hides. Sheep yielded wool. Livestock were also used in ceremonies and given as gifts at births, initiations, and marriages.

▼ THE RICH VS. THE POOR ▼

The number of livestock a person or household owned was an important mark of social status. People without livestock often had to become traders, smiths, or dependents of others to survive.

The bleeding of the cow is part of Maasai custom. The blood is then mixed with milk and drunk by everyone in the *enkang*, including warriors.

Warriors drink a mixture of cow blood and milk as part of
a Maasai custom.

Livestock among the Maasai were not equally
distributed. But the gap between the wealthy, or
il karsisi, and the poor, *il aisinak,* was often
bridged by cooperation. It was common
for the wealthy to lend livestock to poorer
families, who then provided needed labor.

The wealthy Maasai stock owners also hired
outsiders as herders. Some were volunteers
and others were war captives. Those who came
voluntarily from the neighboring communities,
such as the Agikuyu and Luo, usually did so to
get livestock. Some remained among the Maasai
and were gradually adopted. In exchange for
their labor, they were given small herds.▲

chapter

3

SOCIAL STRUCTURE

LIVESTOCK WAS OWNED BY THE FAMILY UNIT and controlled by the male head of the family. This control, however, was not complete. As we have seen, livestock was often lent to others. This meant that several people could hold rights to the same animal. The husband was also expected to give a milking herd to his wife or wives at the time of marriage.

Sons therefore inherited cattle through their mother. The eldest son inherited the remainder of the father's herd when the father died. The youngest married son cared for his mother in her old age and inherited her cattle.

▼ THE ROLE OF MEN ▼

Men's tasks included grazing, watering, and protecting the herd. Men also built enclosures, dug wells, and made weapons, tools, and ornaments.

Every Maasai male is assigned to a group called an age-set, a system that gives him a sense of belonging. Each age-set has clear responsibilities, which creates a sense of identity among the Maasai.

At the bottom of the system are the children, or *inkera*. Before adolescence, boys and girls do minor chores, including herding young animals. Children are taught to respect their elders. They address all adults as "Father" or "Mother." Adolescent boys herd livestock. They are expected to know the herds under their care and to protect them from predators.

The next age-set is composed of boys between the ages of fourteen and eighteen who have been circumcised. Before circumcision, a ceremony called *Alamal Lengipaata* is held, during which the boys receive a new generational name in place of *inkera*, or youth. Circumcision, or *emorata*, marks transition from youth to manhood. The operation is performed by a non-Maasai. The boy is expected to show no sign of pain. Following circumcision he is an *ilmoran*, often translated as "warrior."

The *ilmoran* has become a symbol of what it means to be Maasai. He is expected to be strong and gentle, clever and wise, courageous and confident, and to enjoy both hunting and poetry.

The *ilmoran* live in their own settlements called *emanyata*. There they receive training in

THE NAME-GIVING CEREMONY

Until a Maasai child is five months old, it has only a nick-name. Its official name is given during a special ceremony.

The day before the name-giving, the child's father picks out a ram to have slaughtered for the feast. The meat is roasted, and the right leg is kept aside for use in the ceremony.

On the sacred morning, the baby's head is soaked in milk as a blessing. Its mother shaves off its hair, and then her own. Both of their heads are then smeared with red ochre mixed with the fat of the slaughtered ram.

Because children and cattle are equally important to the fortunes of the Maasai, the name-giving ceremony takes place in the cattle enclosure. Four is a sacred number, so certain rituals use that number to bring good luck to the gathering. The baby's mother closes off the enclosure by placing four branches in the gateway. Then she chooses the most perfect cow from the herd, and milks it four times into a gourd.

Giving the baby a name is a task for one of the community elders. He looks at the baby, then offers a name that seems to fit its personality. All Maasai names have very clear meanings. The parents can decide whether the suggested name is right for their child. If they reject it, the elder offers another. Once a suitable name has been found, the elder blesses the little Maasai. He tells it to live long, to be brave, to respect the poor and unfortunate, and to become as famous as Mount Kilimanjaro.

The gathered friends and relatives all offer their own blessings and spit on the ground to keep evil spirits away from the child. Then the roasted ram is brought out. During the feast the right leg of the ram is presented to the elder. He cracks the bone with an ax and gives the marrow to the child's mother. Removing from the bone what once grew inside it symbolizes the child's entry into the world as a separate person.

cultural and physical skills. Their mothers and younger sisters and brothers live with them and help with house-building, food preparation, and herding. The *ilmoran* are expected to protect their community, livestock, and grazing grounds from intruders. They also carry out cattle raids.

The end of the *ilmoran* period is marked by a spectacular ceremony called *eunoto*. It involves great feasting and dances for the community and special ceremonies for the *ilmoran*. On the last day of the ceremony, the *ilmoran* gather in a large circle at the center of the *emanyata* for blessings from the elders.

Following the *eunoto*, the *ilmoran* return to their fathers' villages. Now they are senior *ilmoran*. Many of them marry at this point.

In another important ceremony called the *olingesherr*, the new senior *ilmoran* receive a permanent group name that moves them into the ranks of junior elders.

The new junior elders now begin to enjoy the privileges of elderhood. They discuss and decide important questions affecting the community. They also possess the power to bless and to curse.

The curse, *ol-deket*, is used only by male elders. It is expected to bring dire consequences. However, it is supposed to work only if the cursed person deserves it.

From junior elderhood, the set is promoted to

The *ilmoran* has become a symbol of what it means to be Maasai.

senior elderhood. Elders include medicine men, spiritual leaders, and judges. They are expected to be wise, disciplined, and hard-working. The most respected and feared elder in Maasai society is the *oloiboni*, the spiritual leader, ritual expert, diviner, and healer.

▼ THE ROLE OF WOMEN ▼

Women are not part of the age-set system but have traditionally played an important role in Maasai economy and society. They did the household chores and cared for the children.

23

Ilmoran or Maasai warriors.

They also tended, milked, and slaughtered animals and took part in herding. They controlled the processing and distribution of milk. They also cultivated crops. As they grow up, girls learn these duties from their mother.

After initiation, a girl shaves her head and begins to dress like a woman, an *esiankiki*. Unlike the *ilmoran*, the newly initiated girls change from youth to adulthood immediately. As prospective wives and mothers, they are expected to lead strictly structured lives. Girls are often married a few months after initiation.

Senior elders include medicine men, spiritual leaders, and judges.

Around the age of eight, both girls and boys have the upper part of their ears pierced. Within two years, their lower lobes are pierced. Wooden plugs or wads of rolled leaves are inserted into the holes to increase the size of the lobes. The Maasai consider large ear lobes to be beautiful.

Girls between the ages of nine and twelve begin to adorn themselves with beautiful necklaces and hides, both decorated with glass beads. They may select boyfriends from among the *ilomoran*.

Between twelve and sixteen, girls may decorate the upper part of their ears with beaded earrings and wear elaborate necklaces. They are not allowed, however, to wear the decorations of an adult woman until they have gone through initiation.

▼ MARRIAGE ▼

Marriage is very important in Maasai society because it solidifies relationships between families. It is arranged in several ways.

In some cases parents choose a wife or husband for their child. A boy's parents might give a gift to a newly married couple, who then promise that if they ever have a daughter she will marry the other couple's son. If they do indeed have a daughter, the parents of the young man continue giving gifts until the girl is initiated.

Sometimes a man chooses his own bride. He declares his interest in a girl by giving her and her parents gifts, usually livestock. If his proposal is accepted, the man and the bride's family begin a long relationship. If he is rejected, any gifts of livestock are returned.

In another form of engagement, a young man takes a friend's sister as his wife. In return, the young man's sister marries the friend.

The man is always expected to make gifts to the woman's family. The gifts, given over a period of time, constitute the *bridewealth*, which is usually cattle. In general, the male elders play the most important role in marriage negotiations because they control the livestock. Sometimes strong women, especially widows, can choose marriage partners for their children.

On the wedding day, the bride is dressed in a

Children are valued highly by the Maasai.

long fine garment and many bead necklaces.
During the marriage ceremony her head is
shaved, and bands of beautiful beadwork are
placed upon it. The bride and groom are
blessed. The guests are served honey beer
brewed from the groom's gifts of honey.

As she leaves her homestead, accompanied
part of the way by her mother and other

Maasai women are responsible for building their houses.

women, the bride cries. Her tears symbolize her sadness in leaving her family. Upon arrival in her new home, she is given gifts by each member of her new family.

Maasai men can have more than one wife. This is called polygamy. In general, wives are much younger than their husbands. Men within the same age-set are not allowed to marry each other's daughters.

Women build and maintain houses. In recognition of women's position in the *enkang'*, houses are regarded as their private property. In fact, a husband is not allowed to enter the house without his wife's permission. Women, therefore, are heads of houses,

A young Maasai girl dressed in her ornaments.

but men are heads of families.

Each wife has her own house and looks after her own children in the homestead.

Children are so important in Maasai society that women hold fertility festivals, moving

from village to village, dancing and praying for children.

During such festivals, the women attack any woman who has had unsuccessful pregnancies and is considered unlucky. If a man is known to mistreat his wife, the women beat him, seize his best cattle, and take away his wife, leaving him to take care of the children and himself.

A mistreated wife often returns to her family. If it is proved that the man was cruel, the marriage is dissolved. Divorce is uncommon among the Maasai. Marriage is not simply a tie between individuals but between families. If a couple have trouble in their marriage, a council of elders discuss the issues at stake and encourage the couple to resolve their differences.▲

chapter

4

NEIGHBORING PEOPLES

IT IS SOMETIMES SAID THAT THE MAASAI WERE the Lords of the Rift Valley, that they terrorized their many neighbors and raided their livestock. Many historians now believe, however, that the Maasai were not really so fierce.

The Maasai's relations with their neighbors were characterized by both cooperation and conflict. Their relations with the many non-Maasai communities living in Maasailand were generally very good. Non-Maasai, generally children, were continually adopted into the society. Many outsiders entered through marriage.

The Chagga people of northern Tanzania were neighbors of the Maasai, but they did not want to expand into Maasailand and therefore posed no threat. When the Maasai economy began to face difficulties toward the end of the

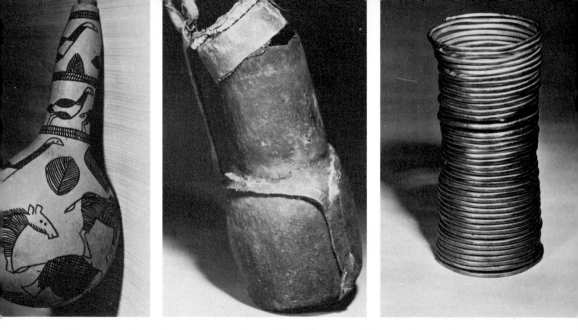

The Maasai bought many products from their neighbors, the Agikuyu, including gourds, iron goods, pots, and baskets.

nineteenth century, valuable trading links were developed between the two groups.

Relations between the Maasai and the Kalenjin were more tense. The Kalenjin lived on the eastern side of Lake Nyanza in Kenya. As they expanded into Maasai lands, the two groups became competitive. However, they still traded and adopted each other's refugees.

Perhaps the most intensive interaction occurred between the Maasai and the Agikuyu. The two societies intermarried, exchanged cultural practices, traded goods, and welcomed migrants. The trade was so important that even in time of war women traders moved freely between Maasailand and Kikuyuland.

In general, the Maasai saw little reason to raid agricultural peoples like their neighbors.

Maasai warriors practicing warfare.

Until the 1880s, the Maasai were an extremely powerful people.

They used to say, "You cannot herd a *shamba* (farm)." As a result, the only people they considered "enemies" and worth fighting were other livestock-keeping Maa-speakers.

Not surprisingly, then, the fiercest conflicts often occurred among the Maasai themselves. Cattle raids and conflicts over pasture and water arose periodically, particularly during droughts. These wars were usually fought between the pastoral Maasai and those who had taken up farming, called the *Iloikop*. The Maasai oral tradition tells of the "Iloikop Wars," which began with a fight over pasture. They ended with the destruction of the aggressive farmers.

One of the most famous of the Iloikop Wars was the Laikipiak War of the 1870s. The defeated Laikipiak left the Rift Valley, which proved to be a mixed blessing for the Maasai. They had triumphed, but they had also become more exposed. Because the Maasai did not have the resources or the manpower to defend the land, other groups expanded into the Rift Valley and challenged Maasai control.

In the meantime, the Iloikop refugees were absorbed into the neighboring societies, where they spread Maasai culture and fighting techniques. The new societies then challenged the Maasai themselves. From the 1880s Maasai power began a swift decline.▲

chapter

5

COLONIAL RULE

IN THE MIDDLE OF THE NINETEENTH CENTURY A great Maasai spiritual leader foretold the coming of Europeans. A flock of white birds, he said, was destined for their land. It would bring devastation, and most of the Maasai people along with their cattle would be destroyed. The venerable seer went on to describe the construction of the Mombasa railway as a great serpent running from the interior to the sea.

For much of the nineteenth and twentieth centuries the Maasai were to remember this prophesy and dread its fulfillment. In 1884 the first European adventurers crossed Maasailand on the caravan routes to the interior. Five years later, after European powers had met in Berlin to divide Africa among themselves, a British military expedition landed on Maasai territory and began seizing the lands that had been assigned to Great Britain.

The Maasai were dispossessed of their land by British colonists during the early twentieth century.

In 1890 an outbreak of a cattle disease called rinderpest, introduced by the invading British forces, killed off most of the cattle of the Maasai, causing widespread hunger and famine. During the same year an epidemic of smallpox and influenza, also brought by the British, killed three quarters of the Maasai nation. By 1904, therefore, following eight devastating years of famine, illness, and death, the British were ready to begin the colonization of the weakened Maasai people in earnest.

The Governor of the East African Protectorate, Sir Charles Eliot, confiscated vast tracts of land from the Maasai and gave them to white immigrants. Two "reserves" were created for them, settlements only a fraction of the size of the original Maasai territory.

Six years later, the Governor ordered the Maasai evacuated from their new Laikipia reserve to another reserve farther to the south.

Legalishu, the most powerful Maasai chief in the Laikipia reserve, protested this latest breach of faith by the British. Together with Lenana, the *laibon* or religious leader of the Maasai, Legalishu met with representatives of the British government to discuss the future of his people and their rights. For several years Legalishu called on the Governor to honor the 1904 treaty that had created the Laikipia reserve. In response, the government threatened to send in

troops if Legalishu refused to move his people
out of the reserve.

Supported by his people and enlisting the
sympathy of two Europeans, Legalishu sued the
colonial government for breach of the treaty.
The Maasai got as far as the Court of Appeal
before the colonial government had the case
thrown out. Legalishu then appealed directly
to the Privy Council in England. This move
alarmed the colonial administrators in East
Africa. Legalishu was warned that his people
would be made to pay dearly if he continued to
oppose the wishes of the white settlers in East
Africa. The Maasai withdrew their case, and in
1910, six years after they had moved into the
Laikipia reserve, the Maasai were once again
dispossessed.

The forced evacuation to the south was hard
on the Maasai. Many of the old people died of
exhaustion. The Maasai also lost thousands of
cattle.

Some 7,000 Maasai and 800,000 head of
cattle, sheep, and goats were transferred to the
southern reserve. The Maasai lost some of their
best grazing lands. This was the beginning of
deliberate government efforts to remove the
resources that the Maasai needed to succeed as
pastoralists.

The Maasai responded to this and to attempts to draft them into the army in a series

The Maasai responded to colonial attempts to draft them into the army by several successful revolts.

of revolts in 1915, 1918, and 1922. After each uprising, the government imposed a heavy fine of 10,000 livestock on all Maasai involved.

A similar attempt was tried in Tanzania by the Germans. The Maasai defeated this plan, but they did lose some land both to European settlers and to African farmers who had voluntarily begun working with the colonial government.

After Germany's defeat in World War I, Great Britain took control of the German colony of Tanzania. In 1926 the new British colonial government created the Maasai District, which covered most of traditional Maasailand. The gov-

ernment claimed that creating the District would
protect the Maasai from losing more land to an
agricultural takeover, but in reality, much of it
was given to European settlers and indigenous
farmers.

In the meantime, the Maasai lost more land
in Kenya to the Agikuyu and other farming
peoples who had also lost land to the European
settlers.

At the same time, European settlers began to
establish commercial cattle ranches and urged
the Maasai to adopt commercial ranching. In
the 1950s the government allowed individual
Maasai to buy and own land for ranching. This
was intended to make the Maasai more productive, but instead it allowed wealthy families to
buy up the best grazing lands.

New game reserves were established on
former Maasai grazing land. Short-cropped
grass once used as pasture was replaced by
scrub and thorn thickets, in which the tsetse and
bush pigs, a favorite host of the tsetse, thrive.
Consequently, areas that had been free of flies
became unsuitable for grazing livestock.

All these changes had a terrible impact on the
Maasai pastoral economy. During colonialism
both the Maasai population and the number of
livestock increased while the land available to
them decreased. The increase in livestock was
partly because of new veterinary services avail-

Despite repression by British colonialism, the Maasai have retained a strong sense of pride and heritage.

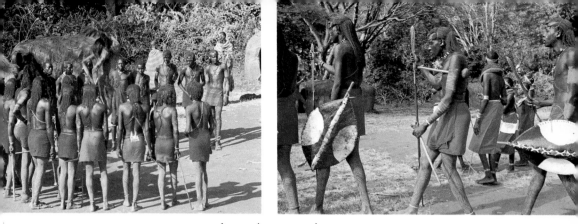

Traditional Maasai dances.

able. The result was overgrazing, which led to soil erosion and destruction of many resources in Maasailand.

The colonial governments became alarmed at the environmental problems and poverty in Maasailand, but the steps they took only made matters worse. For example, the government dug wells and sank boreholes. As herders scrambled to use the new wells, overgrazing became worse.

The government encouraged and sometimes forced the Maasai to sell their livestock and buy new, more productive breeds. But the prices the Maasai received for their cattle were very low and they could not afford the new breeds.

The Maasai were forced into a dependent position by the European colonizers. It was necessary to their survival that they regain independence.▲

chapter

6

INDEPENDENCE

IN 1954, TANZANIA WAS KNOWN AS
Tanganyika. The Tanganyika African Union
(TANU), founded by Julius Nyerere, led the
nationalist movement that won independence
for Tanganyika in 1961. Nearby Zanzibar won
independence in 1963 and joined with Tanganyika to form an independent Tanzania. Nyerere
was president until 1985. Ali Hassan Mwinyi
has been president since then.

Kenya gained its independence largely because of the efforts of former President Jomo
Kenyatta. He was the leader of the Kenya African Union (KAU), formed in 1944 by black
Africans. The KAU led several revolts against
the British. Kenyatta was imprisoned in 1953.
Released eight years later, he led the Kenya
African National Union (KANU) in establishing
full Kenyan independence in December 1963.

Julius Nyerere is still fighting for freedom and equality in Africa.

He served as president until his death in 1978. He was succeeded by his vice-president, Daniel Arap Moi, who still holds the position.

The independent governments of Tanzania and Kenya had similar policies toward the Maasai: They wanted to control Maasai independence and mobility to show that the state had power over all its peoples. Moreover, the state could distribute the benefits of independence and development more effectively.

Like the colonial governments before them, the new African governments hoped to turn the Maasai pastoralists into "productive" sedentary farmers. In 1967 the Tanzanian government declared that rural people would be encouraged to settle in *ujamaa* (villages). It was believed that this system would help the people increase production and have better living conditions. It would also make it easier for the government to provide services such as schools and clinics.

By the mid-1970s millions of peasants had been moved to the *ujamaa*, many of them by force. The peasants were supposed to grow cash crops, which the state would buy at low prices and export at high profit. The peasants resented this, and production began to decline. In the meantime, the government established its own plantations, farms, and ranches.

The pastoralists were also regulated by the

state. First the government concentrated on the
problems of disease and lack of water. Then
it established large-scale, state-owned cattle
ranches on lands traditionally used by the
Maasai and other pastoralists.

Other Maasai lands were taken over to establish wheat farms, settle agriculturalists, and
build military bases. Game parks and reserves
were expanded, and new ones were created.
Several prime grazing lands were then closed to
grazing and settlement. As during colonization,
policies unfriendly to pastoralists were adopted.
For example, the pastoralists were forbidden to
burn grass, a practice that encouraged growth of
good pasture grass. Because the grass could not
be burned, tall, coarse grasses grew. This, in
turn, led to an increase in ticks, which thrive
on such grasses and spread disease.

The Maasai were encouraged to establish
livestock development villages. Like the peasant
farmers, many of the Maasai pastoralists were
forced into the villages. Village life changed the
Maasai life-style. Individuals were allowed to
own only small numbers of livestock, so they
could not support themselves by herding.

The Maasai reponded to the new villages
in several ways. Some moved out to new
rangelands to try to keep their old way of life,
but the government soon followed them there.
Others chose to work with their farming

neighbors by trading their respective products. Some also traded livestock illegally.

In Kenya, more than in Tanzania, large tracts of Maasai lands were also taken over by private interests, both individuals and companies. They started ranches, dairy farms, and cash-crop farms. Expanding cities, such as Nairobi, also moved onto Maasai lands.

Maasai society and economy became more fragile than ever. The gap between rich and poor increased. In Kenya the rural elite set up individual ranches, those less well-off chose group ranches, and the poor people were forced to the cities in search of wage employment.

Most Maasai came to depend on government aid as their land became too small to support the growing population. By the late 1970s, the Kijiado District alone contained 439,370 head of cattle and 701,000 small stock, more than the land could support.

▼ CHANGES IN THE ECONOMY ▼

By 1980 the Maasai controlled only half of the land they had at the beginning of the century. Today the Maasai are among the poorest and most vulnerable people in East Africa. Infant mortality and illiteracy rates are high.

The Maasai tradition of alternate cattle-grazing between pastures has been under enormous strain since the beginning of colonial rule. The

colonial government sought to divide the Maasai people by making boundaries between communities more rigid. And most important, the reduction of grazing land led to the expansion of agriculture.

Two factors have contributed to this expansion. First, as mentioned earlier, many farming peoples moved into Maasai areas. In Kenya, large numbers of Agikuyu and Kipsigis moved into Maasailand. Second, the pastoral Maasai themselves began to farm. Some rich Maasai families even adopted mechanized agriculture to produce wheat and barley. These families often lease out their land or hire laborers to cultivate it. The old system of exchanging livestock for labor between wealthy and poor families is no longer common.

The growth of group and private ranches has changed the way land is owned. Pasture land that was once used by a whole community is now owned by a few private ranchers and farmers. In the old system, whoever lived on the land controlled it. Now a person can control land on which he does not actually live as long as he has title to it.

Water resources, including wells and pools, were once available to all. Now those who control the land sell the water found on it. The government provides water tanks and boreholes, for use of which the Maasai are expected to pay a monthly or yearly fee.

Today it is very difficult for the Maasai to support themselves by cattle herding. Since colonial times they have needed money for taxes, veterinarians, schooling, doctors, and to buy necessary goods. Some have met these demands by selling livestock. But others have been forced to look for wage employment.

Today, tens of thousands of Maasai depend on wage labor for survival. They work on farms and in factories and as security guards. Some are school teachers and university professors, doctors and lawyers. There are also traders, bureaucrats, and soldiers. A few have become important politicians.

Even the Maasai diet has changed. They eat fewer livestock products and more grains. Only the very wealthy can live on milk and livestock products throughout the year. Because of their reliance on government aid during drought, the Maasai have increasingly taken to eating corn and other foods typical of farming peoples. They have also learned to eat foods introduced during the colonial period, such as tea, sugar, potatoes, and bread.

When all is considered, it is remarkable that any group of people could survive such devastation and change. With their traditional ways of living becoming obsolete, the Maasai have the difficult choice of adapting to modern life or becoming an endangered people.▲

chapter

7

POLITICAL AND SOCIAL CHANGES

THE MAASAI HAVE LOST THE POWER TO
govern themselves. The colonial governments
appointed chiefs chosen from the traditional
leaders for the Maasai and other peoples in
Kenya and Tanzania. Since independence, the
governments have chosen leaders from among
educated people. The authority of traditional
Maasai leaders has diminished significantly. Far
more important are the appointed and elected
representatives who have power beyond the local
community.

The age-set system is still important for
many Maasai. But the roles of the age-sets have
changed in some ways. Many youths combine
herding livestock with going to school. In
parts of Maasailand the *ilmoran* continue to
protect livestock, but they are often seen by
governments as potential stock raiders. The

51

MAASAI PROVERBS AND SAYINGS

Like all peoples, the Maasai have sayings that express their particular wisdom and cultural beliefs.

In East Africa, hyenas are considered the toughest of creatures. Therefore, if a man won't give up in a fight, they say "*Etaa embito o-'l-ngojine,*" or, "He is the sinew of the hyena."

People who keep to themselves seem very odd to the Maasai. Of a man who is antisocial they say, "*Erishunye anaa en-gaa o-'shighiria obo,*" meaning, "He keeps himself apart like a sick donkey." (When an animal is sick, it stays away from the rest of the herd.)

"*Ekwenikye 'n-guk in-guruon*" ("The coal laughs at ashes") reminds us not to make fun of an unfortunate person. We may become just as unlucky tomorrow.

Because survival has been such a struggle for the Maasai, it is good to remember that "*Erisyo laikin o kaa,*" or, "Defeat and death are the same thing."

And the community elders say to the young: "*Kinder ol-le-'modai, pe kindoki ol-le-'ngeno.*" "In the beginning we are foolish, but with experience we become wise."

postindependence governments have tried to abolish raiding by doing away with the *emanyata* section of initiation, which they believe trains the *ilmoran* to be aggressive. The *ilmoran* period is now much shorter.

The situation has also changed for the elders. Much of their authority has been taken over by local governments. Land disputes and murder

Much of the power that once belonged to the elders now is held by local governments.

cases are more likely to be decided by the national courts. Cursing, once a powerful weapon used by male elders, is reported to be more frequent but less effective.

Many of the changes in traditional roles in society are caused by Western education. The colonial administration urged the Maasai to go to school and adopt European ways. But on the other, they exhorted them to remain proud pastoralists.

Although most Maasai disapproved of the colonial government's form of education, some began to embrace education itself. In the early 1900s the great *oloiboni*, Olanana, whom the British had made Paramount Chief, showed an interest in colonial education. Through his efforts and those of his brother, Olguris, several attempts were made to set up Christian mission schools in Maasailand. But the mission schools were not as successful as the state schools.

The first state school in Maasailand was established in Narok in 1919. It was financed by taxes on Maasai livestock. In 1926 another school was started in Kajiado. Both schools concentrated on teaching dairy farming. It was believed that the Maasai needed veterinary training to improve their livestock-rearing practices.

Until the 1940s most of the schools were in the administrative centers. Some Maasai pressed the government and the missionaries to spread

By the end of the 1940s many university-educated Maasai became teachers themselves.

education to the more remote parts of the Maasai Reserve. Relatives went to school with the children and took care of the cows they brought. Only fifty students could go to school at once, so that there would be no overgrazing in the school area.

Most of the teachers were European, Asian, or non-Maasai African. By the end of the 1940s there were some university-educated Maasai. Many became teachers themselves.

The curriculum was changed in the 1950s to

put less emphasis on animal husbandry. School enrollment increased. By this time, many educated Maasai had become teachers, clerks, and politicians. Churches established more schools because they saw it as a way to convert students to Christianity.

With independence, the Tanzanian and Kenyan governments spent heavily on education to further economic development and modernization. As a result, there has been a huge increase in educated Maasai. Maasai parents and leaders now consider education necessary for the survival and advancement of their community.

▼ THE POSITION OF WOMEN ▼

Economic and social changes have also affected women and their position in society. Both colonial and postindependence governments were interested in changing the role of women in Maasai society. The colonial authorities and missionaries demanded changes in female initiation rites. As might be expected, the Maasai, including many converts, saw this as an attack on their culture.

During the colonial period, education for girls lagged behind that for boys. Since independence, women have had much greater access. Today, Maasai women are found in many professions, including medicine, law, and politics.

Many educated Maasai women want to

change customs that oppress women, such as female initiation, polygamy, and early marriages. Governments and women's groups have also been trying to discourage such practices and to promote women's position in society.

However, some of the recent changes have not helped rural Maasai women. Private land ownership has encouraged the breakup of the *inkangitie*, or homesteads. Now Maasai homes are only for small family units. Women have become isolated. Tasks such as house-building and child care used to be done collectively, but now each woman must take care of her own home.

The ownership and shape of houses in Maasailand have also undergone changes that have made life more difficult for women. People are much more settled in their residences today, so they often choose to build large brick houses. These houses are expensive and are usually paid for by men. As a result, men regard themselves as owners of houses. Women are thus losing control over an important aspect of Maasai economy and society.

As the Maasai economy has become more commercialized, the sale of livestock has become more common. Women used to take part in trading, but after colonialism, men began to take over market activities. Men also began to manage the large cash income from sales. Women were reduced to trading milk and other livestock products locally and selling items such as firewood, handicrafts, and home-brewed liquor. Today the man decides how to spend the money earned from selling livestock. His decision sometimes conflicts with his wife's or his family's wishes.

Since the market value of cattle has increased, men are not as willing to give cattle as marriage gifts. As we have seen, women as house owners held livestock on behalf of their sons.

Because of their value at market, cattle are less often slaughtered at ceremonies. Women have fewer chances to participate in slaughters, a role that once showed their importance in the pastoral economy.

The age of marriage has also changed for both men and women. Because the *ilmoran* period is shorter, men generally marry younger. This has reduced the number of young women available for older men, making it more difficult for them to practice polygamy. The expansion of education has also contributed to the shortage of marriageable girls. As a result, the pressure has increased on girls who do not go to school to marry at an even younger age.

Divorce in Maasailand is more common than before. Maasai women have become more assertive. Also, many men find it difficult to pay the full bridewealth. A marriage is easier to dissolve if the bridewealth is only partially paid.▲

CONCLUSION

THE MAASAI ARE A FASCINATING PEOPLE WITH a complex and dynamic history. Their culture has undergone many changes in the last two hundred years. They learned from and shared with the various peoples that they came across.

Gradually many aspects of Maasai culture have changed. The Maasai have adapted to new challenges in many ways, with varying degrees of success. Today old customs survive, but in a changed world and often in a changed form. Like other peoples in Kenya and Tanzania, the Maasai have undergone many changes in their long, rich history. There is little doubt that their courage, strength, and pride will help the Maasai adapt, grow, and prosper in the face of the future.

Glossary

Almal lengipaata The ceremony boys undertake just before circumcision.

bridewealth Gifts from a man to his future bride's parents to seal the promised relationship.

emanyata (pl. imanyat) Ceremonial settlement for the *ilmoran*.

emorata The circumcision ceremony that initiates boys into *ilmoran*.

enkang' (pl. inkangitie) Homestead.

Enkidaaroto The Disaster (of the 1880s and 1890s).

esiankiki (pl. isainkikin) Young married woman; bride.

eunoto The graduation ceremony from *ilmoran* into elderhood.

il aisinak Poor man.

il karsisi Rich man.

ilmoran Warrior.

iloshon Section.

inkera Youth.

ol-deket Curse.

olingesherr Ceremony confiming total elderhood.

oloiboni Ritual expert, diviner.

pastoralists People who live by raising livestock.

ujamaa Communal villages.

For Further Reading

Bentsen, Cheryl. *Maasai Days.* New York: Summit Books, 1989.

Boyd, Herb. *African History for Beginners: Part 1—Africa Dawn, A Diasporan View.* New York: Writers and Readers, 1991.

Garlake, Peter. *The Kingdoms of Africa,* rev. ed. New York: Peter Berick Books, 1990.

Jefferson, Margot, and Skinner, Elliott P. *Roots of Time: A Portrait of African Life and Culture.* Trenton, NJ: Africa World Press, 1974.

Saitoti, Tepilit Ole. *Maasai.* New York, Harry Abrams, 1992.

———. *The World of a Maasai Warrior: An Autobiography.* New York: Marboro Books, 1992.

Challenging Reading

Lamb, David. *The Africans.* New York: Random House, 1987.

Moss, Joyce, and Wilson, George. *People of the World: Africans South of the Sahara.* Detroit: Gale Research Inc., 1991.

Saibull, Solomon Ole, and Carr, Rachell. *Herd and Spear: The Maasai of East Africa.* London: Collins and Harvill Press, 1981.

Index

ABOUT THE AUTHOR

Tiyambe Zeleza was born in Harare, Zimbabwe, and grew up in Malawi. He received a master's degree at the University of London and a Ph.D. in history at Dalhousie University, Halifax, Nova Scotia. He has studied and taught at universities around the world. He is currently an associate professor of history at Trent University, Peterborough, Ontario.

Dr. Zeleza is the author of two works of fiction and several historical works, including *A Modern Economic History of Africa: The Nineteenth Century*. He is coauthor of the four-volume *Themes in Kenyan and World History*.

PHOTO CREDITS: AP/Wide World (pp. 44, 55); CFM, Nairobi (all other photos)
PHOTO RESEARCH: Vera Ahmadzadeh with Jennifer Croft
DESIGN: Kim Sonsky

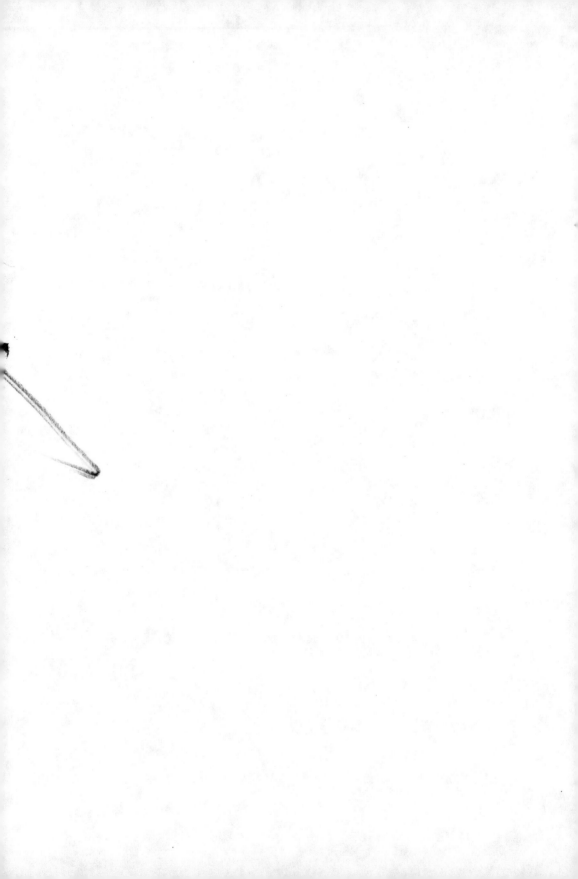